D1807443

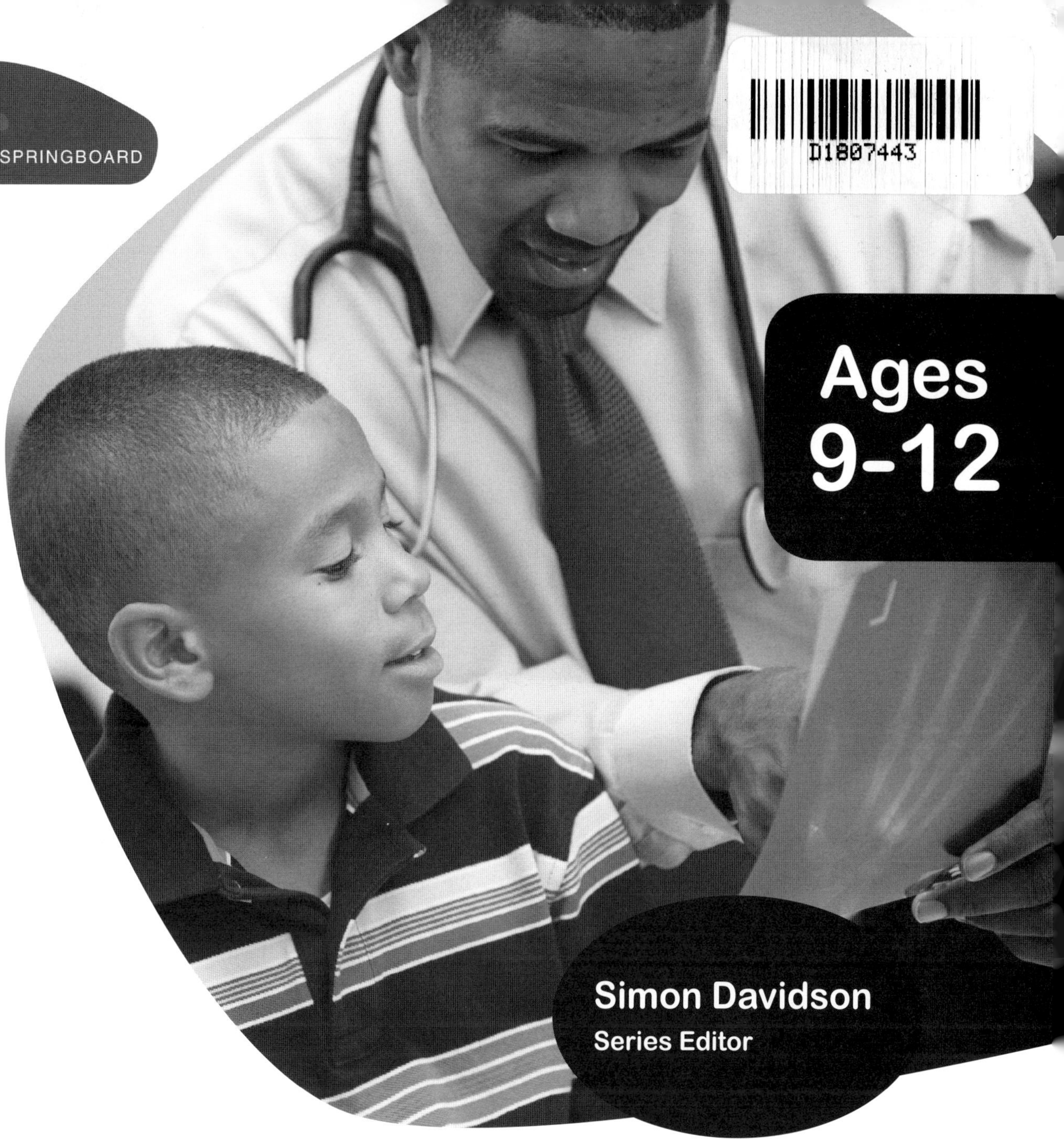

Ages 9-12

Simon Davidson
Series Editor

Helen Saunders and Anne-Françoise Verbert

The World of Work

Teacher's Manual
Inspiring activities and
practical support for delivering
the Primary Years Programme

HODDER
EDUCATION
AN HACHETTE UK COMPANY

The Publishers would like to thank the following for permission to reproduce copyright photographs: page 14 Helen Saunders and Anne-Françoise Verbert
Front cover: © Sean Locke/istockphoto.com

Acknowledgements:
With thanks to the International Baccalaureate Organization® for permission to reproduce its intellectual property. This Teacher's Manual has been developed independently by the publisher and the content is in no way connected with nor endorsed by the International Baccalaureate Organization®.

Page 10 KWL chart adapted from Ogle, D.M. (1986, February). 'K-W-L: A Teaching Model That Develops Active Reading of Expository Text'. *The Reading Teacher*, 39(6), 564–570. doi: 10.1598/RT.39.6.11.

Every effort has been made to trace all copyright holders, but if any have been inadvertently overlooked the Publishers will be pleased to make the necessary arrangements at the first opportunity.

Although every effort has been made to ensure that website addresses are correct at time of going to press, Hodder Education cannot be held responsible for the content of any website mentioned in this book. It is sometimes possible to find a relocated web page by typing in the address of the home page for a website in the URL window of your browser.

Hachette Livre UK's policy is to use papers that are natural, renewable and recyclable products and made from wood grown in sustainable forests. The logging and manufacturing processes are expected to conform to the environmental regulations of the country of origin.

Orders: please contact Bookpoint Ltd, 130 Milton Park, Abingdon, Oxon OX14 4SB. Telephone: (44) 01235 827720. Fax: (44) 01235 400454. Lines are open 9.00–5.00, Monday to Saturday, with a 24-hour message answering service. Visit our website at www.hoddereducation.com.

© Helen Saunders & Anne-Françoise Verbert 2011
First published in 2011 by
Hodder Education, an Hachette UK Company,
338 Euston Road
London NW1 3BH

Impression number	5	4	3	2	1
Year	2015	2014	2013	2012	2011

Illustrations by Peter Lubach
Typeset in 11 on 13pt Frutiger Light by Phoenix Photosetting, Chatham, Kent
Printed in Great Britain by Hobbs the Printers, Totton, Hants

A catalogue record for this title is available from the British Library

ISBN 978 1444 13964 8

Contents

Series overview

The International Baccalaureate® Primary Years Programme (PYP) undoubtedly provides a fantastic education. It encourages students to think creatively and rigorously about very important issues, which can become a lifelong habit. It develops important personality traits, such as being caring and principled. It develops essential concepts, skills and knowledge across disciplines, and the ability to apply them to practical situations. However, it is not an off the peg, ready to teach approach. Teachers have to think thoroughly about all the important elements of the PYP. They have to gather many resources. They have to consider their overall programme of inquiry and the needs of their students. Teachers have to be 'inquirers and thinkers' themselves.

This series sets out to support this process. It provides a manual, which is not designed to be a blueprint, but a guide to help teachers develop their own units. In this series you will not find 'the right central idea' for a unit, or 'the ideal' lines of inquiry. These are not fixed items that can be imported wholesale into every school, just as the PYP is not a fixed body of information to be poured into empty vessels. However, you will find many suggestions to get you started on a new unit and help you reflect on and develop existing units.

In addition there is a collection of books in each inquiry box. This is not meant to be a complete resourcing for the unit, but should complement existing books in schools and be added to according to students' needs and how the unit is developed. The books in each box have been pitched at the general age band for the box, but also include titles that would be suitable for ages above and below. The aim is that the boxes can be used easily across the age bands without restraint of level or age and will accommodate a variety of reading abilities within a class and beyond. Thus I hope that schools will find it easier to prepare for the exciting and continual challenge of developing better units so that students become well-educated global citizens with all the attributes of the learner profile.

Simon Davidson

What is our purpose?

To many students under the age of 12 the world of work will be an unfamiliar environment. They will have heard many comments about work from their families and communities, but their understanding may be limited or superficial. It is important to help students understand what the workplace is all about as they themselves will become part of this world in the future, and because it provides a context for understanding many important aspects of the world around them. They need to have an understanding of the skills required to be a part of a working organisation and how important every role within the organisation is, to ensure that it achieves its purpose. Helping students understand these important issues will encourage them to realise the value of the skills they are learning in school and may explain how their experiences in school are aimed at preparing them for their future in the world of work.

Links to the transdisciplinary themes

How we organize ourselves

'An inquiry into the interconnectedness of human-made systems and communities; the structure and function of organizations; societal decision-making; economic activities and their impact on humankind and the environment.'

© International Baccalaureate Organization®

This unit on *The World of Work* fits in ideally with the theme *How we organize ourselves*. The world of work is a human-made system and people within that system form a community. These organisations have a purpose and everyone within the organisation works together towards a common goal. The actions of working organisations have an impact on our everyday lives and on the world around us. This is an interesting topic for older students to inquire into as their academic experiences may take them closer to a future career in one of those organisations.

This unit focuses on:

- workplaces
- how workplaces are organised and function
- systems needed to ensure goals can be met efficiently
- how work organisations have an impact on the world around them.

Although this unit is primarily planned under the theme *How we organize ourselves*, it can also be adapted to fit into the theme *How we share the planet*. This could be achieved by investigating how organisations manage their responsibility towards the people who work within them and towards the environment. It can also be linked to the theme *Who we are* by exploring communities and their functions and how these have an impact on people's lives.

Younger students can also benefit from an inquiry into the world of work. A unit of this kind can help the students understand the roles and responsibilities of people around them and how these can have an impact on their own lives. If the students have not been introduced to community helpers in earlier years, this might be a good starting point. An immediate example of this may be people who work within the school and how their jobs have an impact on the students. It can also be a good opportunity for the students to inquire into the work their own parents do.

Main ideas of the unit

When you begin to plan a unit of inquiry, you need to start with some broad ideas which will allow you to determine the path your unit will take. Once you have established some of these ideas, your planning team needs to select the main idea you wish to develop into a clearly focused and articulated central idea.

A central idea should be stated clearly in one sentence, and should aim to develop a deeper understanding of elements stated in the transdisciplinary theme. The central idea should be concept-driven, allowing for development of relevant skills appropriate to the intellectual and emotional level of the students. It should build upon and extend the students' prior knowledge by providing opportunities for in-depth inquiry and student-initiated action. Opportunities to explore and utilise students' cultural understanding, awareness and personal experiences should also be provided.

When developing the central idea, you should choose language carefully, avoiding value-laden statements, ensuring that the central idea leads to enduring understanding for life-long learning. You need to be aware that sometimes the central idea will have to be 'unpacked' to ensure all students understand the vocabulary, especially students with learning differences or English Language Learners. The central idea is the initial point for planning but you should ensure that there is sufficient scope within this central idea for student-initiated inquiry and action.

Main ideas from which central ideas could form:

- The world of work is based around human-made systems which support the way we live.
- The workplace is a community with structures and functions which help it operate and achieve its purposes.
- Within the workplace decisions have to be made as a community.
- There are many different roles at work which combine to produce the goods and services we want and need.
- Economic activity in the world of work has an impact on the environment.

Alternative ideas for other transdisciplinary themes:

If this unit were placed under the theme *How we share the planet*, the focus would shift towards an exploration of the rights and responsibilities of work organisations to the human and physical environment:

- Working organisations have to consider their impact on the environment within which they operate.
- Working organisations have a responsibility towards the community where they are situated and towards the global community.
- Equal opportunities are required for all people within the workplace.
- It is often necessary to solve conflicts in order to maintain peace in the workplace.

If linked to the theme *Who we are*, the focus would shift towards an exploration of the human relationships within work organisations and how these organisations affect the individuals within them and those they provide for:

- Human relationships help us to function within the world of work.
- As humans, we have rights and responsibilities within the workplace.
- An individual's personality and talents can influence their choices of career.
- The world of work is directly or indirectly tending to each individual's needs.

Central ideas

The central idea should be a clear statement that reflects a complex understanding of the main ideas behind the unit. It will differ from school to school, depending on the emphasis chosen.

A central idea is a foundation stone to the unit. It should be a powerful, engaging statement which compels people to inquire into the subject. The language should be clear and straightforward, yet intrigue and challenge the ideas of the reader. It should relate to the reader who should feel familiar with the concepts but it should still allow for more in-depth investigation and can be revisited at many conceptual levels. A central idea should be relevant to all students from all cultural, linguistic and economic backgrounds, and encourage them to make connections with their personal experiences.

When generating a central idea, you need to be mindful of many different factors. Firstly, it is recommended that you work collaboratively to share and develop ideas through discussion and from different perspectives. You should refer to the transdisciplinary theme descriptors to ensure that the unit addresses the elements of the theme, contributing to the development of that theme within the school's programme of inquiry. To avoid the unit becoming unmanageable and overwhelming, you should try to keep a clear focus within the central idea and not be tempted to make it too broad. One way to achieve this is to clearly identify the main concepts behind the unit. Finally, the central idea must be assessable and measurable. The assessment must be planned alongside the central idea.

Suggested central ideas for the unit *The World of Work* within *How we organize ourselves*:

- A workplace is a human-made system which serves a purpose.
- The organisational systems within a workplace help people to fulfill their roles.
- Communication is an essential element of a successful organisation.
- Activities of working organisations can affect their local community and environment.
- Many different people collaborate in a workplace to create valuable goods and services.

Suggested central ideas within *How we share the planet*:

- Working organisations have an impact on the environment within which they operate.
- Local organisations and the community are intertwined.
- There are many challenges in ensuring all people have fair opportunities in the workplace.

Suggested central ideas within *Who we are*:

- The world of work is based on human relationships.
- As humans, we have rights and responsibilities within the workplace.
- Our career choices and the way they develop are influenced by who we are and what we can do.
- Individuals are dependent on the world of work.

What do we want to learn?

Key concepts

The key concepts provide the framework around which a unit is built. These concepts are important in helping to shape all inquiries at the heart of the unit. When planning a unit, the focus should be kept on a limited number of key concepts. While most concepts can be addressed within the context of a unit, some will be more relevant and should take priority. As you identify the main key concepts driving the unit, you must revisit the central idea constantly to ensure that the key concept questions are drawing out and are building on the understandings at the heart of the unit. These questions should be broad and open-ended, inviting teachers and students to engage with them. These key concept questions should help inform the lines of inquiry and the teacher questions, as well as the students' own inquiries.

Some ways to generate students questions include:

- Invite the students to work in pairs and explain to each other the role of their parents at work. Encourage the students to question each other to gain more information. The questions and responses can be recorded in writing or in an audio form and collated. Afterwards let the class compare the questions they raised and evaluate whether these same questions are applicable to a range of jobs. These more general questions can then become the students' lines of inquiry.
- Begin by looking together at the school as a workplace, considering the roles of the people who work there and their interactions. The students can then connect the school as a familiar work organisation to other less familiar working environments.

Some of the most relevant key concepts within the context of *The World of Work* unit are identified below:

Form	• What are workplaces like? • What is an organisational system?
Function	• What are the purposes of a workplace? • How are different workplaces organised? • What systems are needed within a workplace?
Connection	• What is the role of workplaces in the local community? • How do people within a workplace collaborate? • How is a workplace connected to the environment?
Responsibility	• What is the responsibility of a workplace towards the individuals within it? • What are individuals' responsibilities to their workplace? • What is the responsibility of a workplace towards its environment?

Possible lines of inquiry

- The world of work
- Systems organised to support the workplace
- Interdependence of workplace systems
- Interdependence of the workplace and the local community
- Interdependence of the workplace and the environment
- Roles within the workplace
- How the world of work fulfills needs.

Teacher questions

- What are 'human-made systems'?
- What are workplaces like?
- What systems are used to organise workplaces?
- What type of communication is needed within a workplace?
- What are different roles within a workplace?
- How do people collaborate at work?
- How are the roles within a workplace interconnected?
- In what ways do workplaces affect the local community?
- In what ways do workplaces affect the environment?

Tips on how to guide lines of inquiry

- Display the selected lines of inquiry in the classroom for students to refer to whenever they need. Suggest they use these to help them develop their own lines of inquiry.
- Alongside these displayed lines of inquiry, encourage the students to post their comments and findings, as they discover information through the various proposed learning engagements.
- Encourage the class to establish a KWL chart to show what they **K**now, what they **W**ant to know and what they have **L**earned (see page 10). Let students add to the **L** section as they inquire and collect information related to their lines of inquiry.
- Form groups of three or four students and ask them to list the people with key roles within the workplace they attend (school). Ask them to establish links between the people, representing their interactions and communications. The students may choose to draw a diagram or to act out the result of their collective ideas sessions.

Key vocabulary

work   workplace   organisation   communication   system   role   rights   responsibility   community   environment   local environment   interdependent   individual   connection   purpose   human-made   conflict   needs   resolution   discussion   decision

Ways of fostering and presenting the students' lines of inquiry

- Ask the students to bring in a photograph or a picture of the working parent they have chosen to discuss. Suggest the students display their questions relating to their parent's role in work around the photograph and use string or colour-coding to link or highlight recurrent questions.
- Ask the students to bring in play figures to represent the various people within the workplace studied. Ask them to label the figures with their names and roles and to connect them with string to represent their interactions. The students can display their questions on the scene in the form of other labels, banners, flags and so on held by the figures.

- Use a learning log for the students to write down their inquiries and record any relevant information or answers they find through learning engagements. A learning log in the form of a small notebook might prove to be useful when recording questions that can then be asked of several different people. You may wish to show different ways of recording several answers to the same questions using pre-made tables or charts, for example.

The World of Work

Name: _____

What I Know

What I Want to know

What I have Learned

How might we know what we have learned?

Assessment opportunities

Assessment is an essential part of the teaching and learning process. It should inform teaching practice in the classroom, as well as provide an insight into the progress the students are making at every stage of the learning process. The assessment process should involve both teachers and students, encouraging them to reflect on their experiences.

When teachers are devising assessment related to the unit, they should constantly refer back to the central idea they have chosen, making sure the assessments are addressing the concept behind the central idea.

This will allow the students an opportunity to:

- show their understanding of what a human-made system means
- demonstrate their understanding of the fact that these human-made systems have a purpose
- identify the roles of individuals within these human-made systems.

Pre-assessment

The following are suggestions to assess the students' knowledge and understanding of workplaces before starting the unit. This is an essential step in the planning process as teachers should aim to build on the students' prior knowledge. Consider using some of the teacher questions from page 9 as a prompt to enable the students to structure their thinking; for example:

- What are workplaces like?
- What systems are used to organise workplaces?
- What are different roles within a workplace?

The students' responses can be recorded in a variety of ways, such as:

- recording their answers to each question in the chart on page 15.
- conducting a survey of the jobs that their parents do and designing a graph or chart to show their results. This survey will lead to a series of new questions for the students to investigate at home. A follow-up survey sheet with suggested questions is provided as a research organiser on page 23.
- cutting out and colouring the paper figure and thought bubble from the sheet on page 31. They should write the job they might like to do when they grow up in the figure and add the reason why they would like that job in the thought bubble. Suggest that English Language Learners draw or represent their ideas in pictures or icons. Create a display and let the students each attach their figures and thought bubbles. Provide some string for the students to link the figures to show connections between the roles.
- using a KWL (what I **K**now, what I **W**ant to know and what I have **L**earned) chart (see example provided on page 10).

Ideas for formative assessment

To help teachers plan further engagements to extend the inquiry at an appropriate level for all their students, formative assessment should be carried out throughout the unit. The following are suggestions to assess students' learning throughout the unit to inform planning and learning engagements.

- As individuals or in interest groups, the students can inquire into jobs they want to find out more about. Provide the books in the inquiry box, other books in the library and Internet access for them to research independently. If possible give them opportunities to interview people in work. Let them share with the class what they discover in a variety of formats, including slideshow presentations, posters, mobiles, dioramas, models, etc. This will lead to a deeper understanding of the central idea for all students.
- Ask the students to prepare tailored questions to interview a guest about their role within a workplace organisation. They can then share the information with the class. With this activity you will be able to assess how much the students understand about what the job entails and what sort of connections it has with other roles within or outside of the workplace.
- Arrange the students in groups with a common interest and ask them to write a role-play representing the communication between people within a workplace. Ask the students to refer to the information gathered in their research and interviews to create a role-play as close to reality as possible. As the unit evolves and the students gain more knowledge, ask them to revisit and modify the scenes as necessary, explaining to the class what changes they have made and why.
- Invite the students to identify the ultimate purpose of a workplace. Once they have identified this, suggest they investigate the various tasks each person involved in this workplace must carry out in order to help achieve the purpose. Use the school as a model of a workplace, as all students will then have experience of a human-made system. Use copies of the sheet provided on page 32 to organise this learning engagement.

Assessment tips

Ongoing formative assessment can be kept and recorded in various ways. Any data you gather should be considered at every stage of the inquiry as a means of informing you of the next steps required for your students to understand the central idea.

- Make anecdotal observations about students' engagement, participation and contributions on sticky notes. These sticky notes are ideal to collect into a record book at the end of the day to form part of an assessment.
- Ask the students to write their comments on what they have learned or enjoyed on the interactive whiteboard. They can be saved and be revisited at a later time.
- Scribe briefly what the students are sharing during group discussions. Add these notes to your record book and use them when planning the next steps of the unit or when writing assessment reports.

- Use checklists during activities; this is particularly useful when the students are working towards an assessment or following a series of instructions. It helps to keep the students focused and mindful of the expectations; for example, a checklist could list the requested criteria for a piece of work such as 'I applied what I learnt before', 'I researched all the questions, 'I gave justifications for my opinions', and so on.

Ideas for summative assessment

The main aim of summative assessment is to give teachers, students and often parents a clear understanding of what students have learned. This should be a culmination of the teaching and learning of the unit and should be documented using appropriate tools. The summative assessment task chosen should directly assess the students' understanding of the central idea. Make the criteria for assessment clear prior to the activity, possibly by creating a rubric with the students. You must ensure that the assessments proposed address the different learning preferences of each individual. A summative assessment suggestion for each proposed central idea is given below.

- **A workplace is a human-made system which serves a purpose:** Ask the students to choose a workplace they have been investigating. Invite them to identify the various roles within that workplace, the skills required from each role, how they interconnect and how they contribute towards achieving the purpose of the organisational workplace. Give the students the choice about how they will represent this information – as a piece of writing, oral presentation, slideshow, picture, poster, diagram or 3-D model and so on.

- **The organisational systems within a workplace help people to fulfill their roles:** Suggest that as a class the students identify a project that could come to life in their school. It could be opening a shop at break time, organising a recycling system and so on. Ask each student to identify the purpose of their project, the main roles within the project and how they fit together, to write their job description, identify the people they need to communicate with, use different methods of communication (email, face-to-face meetings and so on) and take and share minutes of their meetings. Use the sheet on page 30 to organise the plans. Let students carry out the projects and complete a reflection on the process: What were the challenges and successes and the learning outcome, and what are the modifications they would make were they to do it again?

- **Effective communication is an essential element of a successful organisation:** Select an example of a purpose that must be achieved; for example, within the school or a place the students are familiar with. This could be organising hot lunches, an assembly, attendance-keeping, bus rides and so on. Identify all the instances where communication is required and the types of communication that are to be used. Imagine a breakdown of communication at different levels and what the implications would be. How can the communication breakdown be fixed or replaced? If the students work in groups on different scenarios, give them an opportunity to compare their findings to identify similarities and differences.

- **Activities of working organisations can affect their local community and environment:** Ask the students to identify a local workplace in their immediate school environment. Let them identify the service provided and the positive and negative impacts it has on the local community and on the environment: issues with parking, rubbish, noise, employment, meeting a need, convenience and so on. Give the students the choice of how to present their findings, such as with a slideshow, recording interviews with neighbours, writing a newspaper article and so on.

- **Many different people collaborate in a workplace to create valuable goods and services:** Suggest the students consider a workplace, such as their school, and think about all the different roles and people who work there. Ask them to make connections between the different departments and how they fit together to provide the overall service; for example, how the lunch-time cooks must work with the supervisors to provide the whole lunch-time experience for students.

Assessment criteria for the unit

Depending on the central idea, the criteria for assessment could be that students:

- recognise that everyone has their own range of skills
- realise that effective communication is needed to achieve a common goal
- understand that people choose or are chosen for a particular job or role according to their personal skills
- understand some of an individual's rights and responsibilities within a workplace
- understand that workplaces have a positive and a negative impact on the environment and community.

Assessment good practice

Assessment is essential at all stages of inquiry and should be as varied as possible. Below are some ideas for assessment of different stages of the inquiry, including assessment of prior knowledge, formative assessment that will inform the next steps of the inquiry and summative assessment at the end of the process. The suggestions include both individual and group assessments.

Following a long series of activities and thorough planning, the students finally get on with the realisation of their project. Their mini-business is underway (right) and everyone has a precise role and a task to achieve to reach the goal. Here, they are shown preparing advertisements for the upcoming event. The success will be measured by the response they get to their business. The students will be able to assess the success of their team and also their own contributions.

During a group visit to a workplace (left), the students gather information through their observations and their inquiries. They have an opportunity to ask the questions they prepared in class. The responses can be used as a tool to assess the quality of the questions.

Students and teachers have organised a day at work with one of the parents (right). The students have prepared questions and the parents have been prompted to help the students understand their role and place within an organisation or a community. Students are encouraged to take notes and bring them back to use in further activities. This type of engagement occurs early in the unit and can be used as a pre-assessment, helping you gather information on the students' understanding of the central idea.

The students act out a script they have prepared together in groups or pairs (left). This follows their inquiry into roles within a workplace and must represent the interactions between two or more people at the workplace. This engagement can be used as a summative assessment of the students' understanding of the central idea.

Name: _____

The World of Work

What is a workplace?

How does a workplace function?

What roles might people have within a workplace?

How best might we learn?

Tuning-in activities

- Invite the students to investigate their parents' work and bring in any objects, photographs or articles relating to their parents' jobs.
- Give the students an opportunity to explore the school as a workplace.
- Invite the students to browse through selected materials, including books, photos, videos, DVDs, etc.
- Encourage the students to generate and record their own questions.
- Invite guest speakers from a range of different job roles in the community to ignite the students' interest.

Start your inquiry from the students' own experience of the world of work, which may be limited to school, shops, public facilities such as sports grounds, cinemas and restaurants. They may also have second-hand knowledge of their parents' job roles. Make sure you emphasise that every job has a purpose and is important in the global organisation of the workplace and in its interconnections with the environment. Encourage the students to be sensitive towards others and show respect towards the roles being discussed. As a teacher, you need to encourage the students not to view certain jobs as being more important than others.

Ideas for learning engagements

1 What do your parents do at work?

Key concepts: Form: What does my parents' workplace look like? Function: What is their role within the workplace? Connection: How are they connected to other people in the workplace?

Transdisciplinary skills: *Communication skills:* Expressing ideas clearly and stating opinions. *Thinking skills:* Gaining facts and ideas, making use of knowledge and seeing relationships between ideas.

Activity ideas: The students will consider what they think their parents' jobs are all about and what they actually do in work every day. Ask them each to choose one of their parents who has a job (if a student does not have a working parent, you may ask them to choose another person they know, even yourself, to complete the activity). Invite the students to write and/or draw pictures to explain what they believe their parent does in work on a daily basis. These contributions could be compiled into a class book about the various roles of the people chosen or used to create a wall display. After their initial thoughts have been recorded, ask the students to conduct interviews or visit their parent's workplace to find out more information about what they actually do. They can record this information in the same way and compare their findings with the initial thoughts.

Assessment ideas: This could provide an ideal opportunity to assess students' prior knowledge on the world of work. The activity will provide a good picture of the students' understanding of the world of work and what people do in various roles every day. You may want to scribe students' comments on the whiteboard or poster sheet to remember what was shared. Sticky notes can also be used to add to your record book. It will give you a good idea of the level of the students' understanding of roles in the workplace and ideas of engagements needed to develop further the students' understanding of the world of work.

2 Job questionnaire

Key concepts: Form: What is a workplace? Function: What is the purpose of a workplace? How is a workplace organised? Connection: How is a workplace connected to the local community and to the environment? How are people within a workplace connected to each other? What systems are needed within a workplace? Responsibility: What responsibilities do various roles within the workplace carry?

Transdisciplinary skills: *Social skills:* Showing respect for others and understanding of different perspectives, working cooperatively and politely. *Communication skills:* Recording questions in an understandable format. *Self-management skills:* Knowing and applying appropriate codes of behaviour. *Research skills:* Formulating relevant questions in order to carry out inquiries and interviews.

Activity ideas: In this activity, students will prepare questions to ask various adults in order to gain a better understanding of the adults' roles within their workplaces. Ask students to work alone, in pairs or in small groups to formulate questions to be asked in interviews with parents, other visitors or when they are visiting a workplace. Guide the students' thinking by providing appropriate key concepts which they should address during the interview. They will need to record their questions clearly, in a standard format that can be used repeatedly.

Assessment ideas: This is a good opportunity for formative assessment, as the questions identified by the students should indicate the level of understanding they have about various aspects of the workplace. Once you have reviewed the students' questions, it may be useful to make notes about students who need further guidance. If the questions are still very superficial or do not address appropriate material, you may need to intervene and work with the students to formulate questions, possibly by modelling how you would respond to these questions. This may help them to identify any weaknesses in their own questions.

3 Going to work

Key concepts: Form: What is the workplace? Function: What is the purpose of this workplace? How is it organised? What systems are used here? Connection: How is this workplace connected to the local community? How are people within this workplace connected to each other? Responsibility: What responsibilities do the people within this workplace have towards one another?

Transdisciplinary skills: *Social skills:* Showing respect for others, working cooperatively and politely. *Communication skills:* Recording information in writing, paraphrasing, taking notes, presenting findings in an appropriate form. *Self-management skills:* Planning and carrying out activities effectively, knowing and applying appropriate codes of behaviour. *Research skills:* Formulating relevant questions, gathering information, recording information in a variety of ways.

Activity ideas: To gain some direct experience of the workplace, help the students to organise a visit to the workplace of their parent or another adult in the school community. You may need to get permission for them to be absent for a day and they will need to write a letter or email requesting permission to visit. Help the students identify questions they would like answered or areas of interest they have in advance of the visit. Discuss methods of recording the information they gather beforehand too. Following the visit, students should record the information they gather in an appropriate way in order to share with the class. This may be in the form of drawings, photographs with captions, writing, a slideshow, posters and so on.

Assessment ideas: This is a useful formative assessment. Provide a checklist of criteria for the visit, to include information the students need to find and different tasks they need to complete whilst on the visit, such as gathering some evidence in the form of artefacts or information sheets. The students' responses to the visits will indicate their level of understanding of the systems in place and the role of the people they met at the workplace.

4 Tell me about your job

Key concepts: Function: How is a workplace organised? Connection: How are people within a workplace connected to each other?

Transdisciplinary skills: *Research skills:* Observing using all the senses to notice details. *Self-management skills:* Knowing and applying appropriate codes of behaviour in various situations such as the workplace. *Communication skills:* Listening to others in order to gather information.

Activity ideas: Plan and organise a group visit to a nearby work organisation to explore the different roles people have and the connections between those roles. Choose a place that presents a variety of roles and a sufficient number of workers (for example, a supermarket) to provide variety and allow the students to inquire in groups in different areas. Ask the students to make observations and plan for some specific questions to different people at various levels of the system (for example, checkout person, department manager, overall supermarket manager). The students might take notes, photographs or film if permitted. Try to include an opportunity to meet managers who might be able to provide some documents representing their organisational system.

Assessment ideas: This type of activity does not call for an assessment but is an opportunity for the students to reflect on what they have discovered and possibly identify with one of the roles encountered. As an observer, such a trip is a type of formative assessment; the students' interest and participation will inform how to plan the rest of your unit.

5   Roles within our school

Key concepts: Form: What systems are in place within the school? Function: How is the school organised? Connection: How are people within the school connected to each other? How is the school connected to the local community and to the environment? Responsibility: What are your responsibilities within the school?

Transdisciplinary skills: *Social skills:* Showing respect for others and understanding of different perspectives, working politely. *Communication skills:* Speaking clearly, listening attentively, recording information in writing, paraphrasing and taking notes. *Self-management skills:* Knowing and applying appropriate codes of behaviour. *Research skills:* Formulating relevant questions, gathering information, recording information.

Activity ideas: Invite the students to interview various people who work within the school to build a picture of how the school works as an organisation. Ask them to use prepared questions to interview a range of people who contribute to the life of the school about the roles they fulfil. Provide copies of the sheet on page 23 to organise their questions and record notes. They could also use audio or video equipment to record their interviews. Having recorded the written and audio interviews, help the students to use the information they find to make a display demonstrating how the school is a working organisation, the connections between those who work within it and the interactions within the school.

Assessment ideas: This can be used as a formative assessment to build upon the students' understanding of one work organisation. They should be able to transfer their understandings gained in this activity to other situations and workplaces, as well as transfer the skills required to carry out interviews when continuing their research.

6   Life-size workers

Key concepts: Form: What is the role of a 'secretary'? Function: What skills are necessary for this job? Connection: How does this person relate to others within the workplace? Responsibility: What is the responsibility of this person within their workplace?

Transdisciplinary skills: *Thinking skills:* Making decisions about possible career choices based on criteria identified and according to their personality. *Communication skills:* Constructing visuals to share ideas and information. *Self-management skills:* Spatial awareness.

Activity ideas: After engaging in research on a variety of jobs, invite the students to identify the one job they might like to have. Provide them with large sheets of paper and ask them each to make a life-size paper worker. Show them how to take it in turns to lie down on the large sheets of paper and ask a friend to draw around them, and then cut out their paper character. They can use the paper figures to write in the information they have gathered about the job chosen. Depending on the job, the students can write or draw any necessary equipment; for example, for a bricklayer they could draw or cut out pictures of a spirit level and a trowel. Suggest that the students display their figures and see how they could connect with each other, grouping other building workers with the bricklayer, for example.

Assessment ideas: Depending on when this activity is proposed in the unit, it can be used either to show the students' knowledge before the inquiry or to demonstrate how much they have learned up to this point. It can also be used to assess the growth of the students' knowledge if you invite them to add information as the unit progresses, asking them to use different colours to identify prior knowledge and knowledge gained.

7 Start your own business

Key concepts: Function: How can we make our mini-business work? Connection: How can this mini-business connect to the school community? Responsibility: What is the responsibility of each person within the business?

Transdisciplinary skills: *Communication skills:* Asking questions clearly, recording information and presenting findings. *Research skills:* Formulating questions, gathering information, recording and sorting data, gathering information from a variety of first- and second-hand sources such as books, people, documents, etc. *Self-management skills:* Planning and carrying out activities effectively. *Social skills:* Understanding the importance of assuming responsibility, being courteous in group discussions and taking turns.

Activity ideas: Suggest the students organise a mini-business within the school to offer a service to the school community. This is a long-term engagement which will go on beyond the length of the unit. It requires long-term commitment and is intended to give the students a true experience to prepare them for the world of work. Guide the students to identify a need within the school that could be answered with a project/business; for example, selling healthy snacks during break time, managing small play equipment for breaks and so on. When they have identified the purpose of their mini-business and this has been agreed by the head of the school, encourage the students to list all the roles that are necessary and the tasks that each role must carry out. They should also identify other people within the school who they will need to communicate with. Help guide the students to take on roles that best suit their talents and skills. You will need to ensure that the school is supportive of this project before launching it, in order to avoid disappointment and the whole project collapsing or failing to take off.

Assessment ideas: This engagement provides multiple opportunities for assessment; each stage of the elaboration (such as identifying roles, choosing roles and communicating with others, and of the development of the project) is subject to reflection. The concrete result, the 'business', is material for assessment in itself. As long as it runs, the project must be re-evaluated and adapted according to the students' observations to evolve the project fully.

8 Organisations and the environment

Key concepts: Connection: How is a workplace connected to its environment? Perspective: Which effects are positive, negative or a mixture? Responsibility: What is the responsibility of a workplace towards its environment?

Transdisciplinary skills: *Research skills:* Formulating questions, observing things around us, gathering information, recording data. *Self-management skills:* Making informed choices about the way we behave.

Activity ideas: Together explore the environmental impact of a work organisation, such as the school, and find out how the workplace takes steps to minimise its impact. This engagement will last for several sessions and will involve a series of activities. To start, help the students generate a list of possible impacts an organisation may have on its environment. Draw their attention to the fact that the impact can be either positive, negative or a combination of both. This list will help the students formulate targeted questions to ask people in the environment, such as neighbours, shops, caretakers and so on. Allow the students opportunities to inquire into different areas within and outside the workplace. This might include a chance for some of them to walk around the premises to identify possible impacts and take photographs as appropriate. Back in class, ask the students to organise and present the data they have recorded. Provide time for a phase of reflection for the students to make suggestions on how to minimise the negative impacts and follow this by some direct action if appropriate.

Assessment ideas: The data the students present can be used as an assessment of their understanding of responsibility and of their capacity to analyse a situation. It is important not to assess only the presentation skills, but also to focus on the content. Encourage students to explain the process of their inquiry and the reasons for their conclusions.

9   In my town

Key concepts: Function: What is the purpose of a workplace? Connection: How are workplaces connected to the local community and to each other? Responsibility: What is the responsibility of a workplace towards its environment and community?

Transdisciplinary skills: *Research skills:* Formulating questions, gathering information, recording data. *Communication skills:* Listening, speaking clearly and asking questions, viewing and interpreting visuals. *Thinking skills:* Looking at organisational systems and finding their components, identifying relationships between them.

Activity ideas: Undertake a project together to gather information about various work organisations in your local area. Ask students to consider what needs they address and how they are linked. Start by identifying an area near your school which offers a range of workplaces such as a doctor's practice, shop, chemist and so on which are familiar to the students and which are approachable. Invite the students to suggest what the purpose of these workplaces might be and how they might be linked. Encourage them to organise a meeting with representatives from the workplaces and help them formulate questions to confirm their suppositions and to find out more information. Let the students share their findings through a variety of forms such as posters, visual diagrams, photographs, clips of interviews, audio recordings and so on.

Assessment ideas: The formulating of questions is a good formative assessment tool as it will inform you of the students' understanding of the central idea. How the students present their findings can also be used as an assessment and can be measured using a rubric, a peer assessment or a personal reflection. As always, it is important that the students are clear on the criteria early on in the engagement to give them the best chance to perform with the goal in mind.

10   My future job

Key concepts: Form: What is the workplace/job? Function: What skills are needed to be successful at this job and in this workplace? Connection: How do people within a workplace interact and communicate? Perspective: Which jobs would I like to do?

Transdisciplinary skills: *Research skills:* Formulating relevant questions, gathering information, sorting and categorising information. *Thinking skills:* Gaining ideas, seeing relationships between ideas, making judgements based on criteria.

Activity ideas: Ask the students to identify a job they believe they would like to do when they leave school and invite them to research this job using various sources including the books from the inquiry box, other available books, the Internet and through interviewing others. Explain that the students will need to identify the key aspects of the job and the skills needed to be successful in that job. They can record the information they uncover in any way they wish including written, diagrams, posters and slideshows and can then reflect on what they have discovered. Let them consider whether their own personal skills and attributes suit the job they have chosen and help them to identify areas which they could develop in preparation for this career path. You can use the research sheet on page 31 to support this activity.

Assessment ideas: This can be an excellent formative or summative assessment opportunity. The students should be able to show that they have identified and researched a job, that they understand what the job requires in terms of skills and personal attributes and then use this information to decide whether they are suited to this job. A rubric should be given to the students in advance so that they are aware of the criteria identified.

Disciplinary concepts

Social Studies aspects

Students will have the opportunity to inquire into human systems and economic activities, social and cultural organisations, resources and the environment.

- Through studying different workplaces, the students will begin to understand how and why we need organisation and systems.
- When investigating interconnections in workplaces, the students will begin to understand the importance of communication in achieving a shared purpose.
- Through an exploration of a local workplace, the students will gain an understanding of the impact of a workplace on its local community and on the environment.

Language aspects

Language aspects will be present within every unit of inquiry, both as a means of learning and as a means for the students to express their understanding and ideas. The following are suggestions for developing specific skills in all areas of language:

- **Listening:**

Gathering information from guest speakers; collecting information from interviews.

- **Speaking:**

Presenting and comparing findings at group sharing times; joining in class discussions, sharing ideas; family discussions.

- **Reading:**

Book research using non-fiction texts; gathering information from other sources such as job descriptions, procedures, meeting agendas and minutes; looking at job advertisements and the language they use.

- **Writing:**

Taking notes during guest-speaker presentations; making notes of important ideas from discussions with parents or workers; forming questions; writing job advertisements, using engaging language.

- **Viewing and presenting:**

Making posters, displays, slideshows, etc. to share findings; exploring web pages; making and interpreting charts and visuals.

Personal, Social and Physical Education aspects

The exploration of *The World of Work* will allow the students to reflect on their personal skills and attributes that will be useful and help them succeed in the workplace. They will begin to appreciate the importance of interactions with other people in order to achieve a purpose. Inquiring into different roles within the workplace will help the students realise that each role carries different responsibilities but that they are dependent on one another to be successful. This is also a good opportunity to explore the impact of familiar organisations on the community and the environment. Group activities will help students to appreciate the importance of communication skills when working together.

They will have the opportunity to:

- explore their own place and the role of their parents within the world of work
- reflect on their own skills and how they may be useful in their future choice of career
- understand the importance of interaction and communication within the workplace
- investigate the responsibilities associated with different roles
- appreciate the impact of a workplace on the environment.

Transdisciplinary skills

Whilst this unit is concept driven, it is also important to recognise the value of transdisciplinary skills. These core skills help students to learn through all areas of the curriculum and can be applied to many different situations both in and out of the classroom. These skills should not be taught in isolation but will become part of the authentic learning experience.

Depending on the central idea that teachers choose, and depending on the focus of the unit, it may become apparent that some transdisciplinary skills are better addressed than others. This needs to be considered in the planning stages of the unit. Possible opportunities to use transdisciplinary skills are listed below.

Thinking skills

- Looking at an organisational system and finding its components, identifying relationships between them.
- Drawing meaning from ideas learnt and communicating understanding.
- Making decisions about possible career choices based on criteria identified and according to their personalities.

Social skills

- Showing respect for all roles and understanding of different skills and preferences.
- Understanding the importance of assuming responsibility.
- Being courteous in group discussions and taking turns.

Communication skills

- Reading a variety of sources for information and understanding what has been read to draw conclusions.
- Recording information in writing, paraphrasing, taking notes.
- Listening to others in order to gather information (interviews).
- Speaking clearly and asking questions articulately.
- Understanding organisational charts and graphs.
- Constructing visuals and multimedia to share ideas and information.

Self-management skills

- Planning and carrying out activities effectively.
- Knowing and applying appropriate codes of behaviour in various situations such as the workplace.

Research skills

- Formulating relevant questions in order to carry out inquiries and interviews.
- Gathering information from a variety of first- and second-hand sources such as books, people, documents, etc.
- Observing using all the senses to notice details.
- Recording information in a variety of ways such as note-taking, charts, tallying.
- Sorting and categorising information into understandable formats.
- Choosing different and appropriate ways to present findings throughout this unit.

Name: _____

Research organiser

Interview conducted by: _____

Person interviewed: _____ Role: _____

What company do you work for?

What is your role within the company?

What does the role involve?

What other people or departments do you work with?

What communication tools or skills do you use?

What other companies do you work with?

What does a typical day at work involve?

PYP attitudes

A selection of attitudes will be developed through the inquiry into *The World of Work*. These attitudes are important in all aspects of life and are imperative to establish at a young age to enable our students to function and succeed in the world of work later in life. Some of the most relevant attitudes in this unit are listed below, but teachers may decide to focus on other attitudes as they plan their own focus and central ideas.

Commitment

Students will gain a better understanding of the importance of their role within an organisation and how they must each as individuals take their role seriously to allow the community to achieve its purpose.

Confidence

Students will be encouraged to reflect on their strengths and to think about how these can be applied in different situations to contribute to a common purpose.

Cooperation

Students will show understanding that they must adjust their behaviour and decisions as the situation demands in order to collaborate and cooperate.

Enthusiasm

Students should realise the importance of willingly putting effort into everything they do.

Respect

Students will be encouraged to show an understanding of other people's work and how everyone in the workplace depends on each other. This will help students develop a greater awareness of responsibility in the workplace.

Tolerance

Exploring the diversity of roles in the workplace will contribute to developing a greater understanding of the importance of each individual role. This will help and support the students to gain an increased acceptance of people and situations that are less familiar.

Links to the learner profile

Inquirers	Students investigate and gather information using the necessary skills independently.
Communicators	Students use a variety of modes of communication to work effectively in collaboration with others.
Principled	Students show respect for themselves, others and the communities around them. They take responsibility for their own actions and recognise the consequences.
Reflective	Students are able to identify their own strengths and limitations when considering their personal development.

What resources need to be gathered?

Resources and the classroom environment

The students and their families should be the main source of information at the beginning of the unit. The school environment will also be a useful model to investigate workplaces. As the unit progresses, other resources will be used to enrich the students' knowledge and understanding.

- Students can use their parents as a source of information: encourage them to speak to their parents about the work that they do and what their roles involve in order to share this information with the class. You should help the students to identify similarities and differences between their parents' roles as well as obvious links.
- Encourage students to bring in photographs of their parents at work, objects that they might use, articles about their work and other relevant materials that can be used for a display.
- Collect together many books: the books from the inquiry box are a good start, but as wide a range of books as possible should be placed on display in the classroom. They should be inviting to the students so that they look inside, read around the subject and begin to gather information. Ensure that the books do not all focus on one area as this will influence the students' thinking.

- Guest speakers: having people from the local community share their experiences in the world of work is an asset that must be taken advantage of. Giving the students the opportunity to learn about different roles and workplaces from those who have experienced it first-hand is a good approach.
- Visits to a parent's workplace or to a local organisation can give the students first-hand experience of working systems in action.

Other useful resources

- Books: a wide range of non-fiction titles, starting with the inquiry box
- Posters and photographs of workplaces or students' own representations of workplaces or roles (e.g. doctors/plumbers/shopkeepers)
- Resources from the local community, including staff at school, parents and locally employed workers
- Cameras
- Audio-visual recording equipment
- DVDs/videos of people at work or of interviews with people about their jobs
- ICT resources (including email, word processing, graphing programs)
- Local workplaces: visits and as contact for guest speakers
- Local neighbourhood businesses or organisations.

Aspects for English Language Learners

Expression through means other than language

The World of Work unit can be made accessible for students who are learning the language of instruction. In order to support and engage those students, it is important to begin with their own experiences and the ones of their families and friends in a very concrete way. The students can carry out their investigations of their parents' workplaces in their own language and could use people in the school community to help them translate what they learnt. Any questioning or interviewing must be prepared in class and an opportunity must be given to English Language Learners to have their questions translated from the language with which they are comfortable.

Use of the mother tongue in learning

Wherever and whenever possible, an open-minded teacher will allow students operating in a language other than their mother tongue opportunities to break free of language constraints and work in their first language. Obvious opportunities may be conducting interviews with family members or guest speakers. Allowing students who share a mother tongue to work cooperatively in their own language can also be very liberating and can uncover a depth of understanding previously undiscovered. The teacher may need help from other students, teachers or parents to translate, if necessary.

Ways for parents to support learning

Another valuable way of supporting English Language Learners is to enlist parental support in their mother tongue. Parents should be encouraged to discuss ongoing inquiries with their children in their own language. If parents are provided with lists of essential vocabulary and an outline of the unit, they should be able to help translate key words and ideas. Encouraging parents to share support materials in their own language will allow students to read and understand concepts and begin to transfer their understanding within the context of the language they are learning.

Basic linguistic support

The teacher will be able to support English Language Learners by:

- enriching the vocabulary needed to understand and discuss the workplace
- introducing or reinforcing the interrogative form
- providing access to translating programs on the Internet
- pairing students with someone who shares their mother tongue but has the ability to communicate in English already.

Supporting and extending students with learning differences

Supporting

As for the English Language Learners, this unit provides ways for students with learning differences to express themselves. The unit allows for multiple opportunities for communication, starting with discussions at home. This should give the students with learning differences a chance to build their confidence. Students should feel free to experiment with different ways of communicating in order to find new ways of expressing their understanding.

Some support in the following areas will help students gain comfort during the activities proposed within this unit:

- note-taking to collect data during interviews or presentations
- thinking and formulating questions for interviews.

Sometimes it may be possible to elicit support from the wider school community. Parents may be able to support their child at home by reading materials to them and discussing the main ideas. Similarly, other students may provide support in class by sharing their knowledge, or students with learning difficulties may be paired up with more able students. It may also be possible to provide a learning buddy in the form of an older student who can help provide support and 'coach' a student experiencing difficulties.

Many students in need of support may be experiencing language and communication difficulties, possibly when reading or expressing their ideas. To support these students, it is vital that a range of books and stimulus materials are found at a level appropriate for their language skills. It is also important that the teacher is able to show these students that they are free to express their ideas without worrying about making errors in speech or in writing. It should be stressed at all times that it is the ideas that are important, not the mode of expression. This is especially important when assessing a student's work.

In order to provide all students with an opportunity to be successful, teachers must be mindful of providing assessment opportunities to suit all students. When planning assessments it should be possible to have clear objectives about what the outcome of the assessment should be whilst giving students the freedom to approach the task in different ways and express their understanding in a mode which suits them. Approaching the assessment through the lenses of different learning styles may help ensure that the task is accessible to all.

It is also vital to students who need support that the expected outcome of the assessment task is clear from the very beginning. Indeed, this is good assessment practice in any context. Teachers should provide the criteria for success in the assessment task from the beginning. This will help all students, especially those who need support, to recognise what they are aiming for. It may be possible to create assessment tools with the students, so that they help to define the criteria for success and begin to visualise what they need to do to be successful. If samples of work from previous years are available as benchmark pieces, they may be a very concrete way to demonstrate what the teacher's expectations are at every level.

Extending

Many of the ideas in this unit require research about workplaces and roles of people within workplaces. More able students will very quickly make connections with information they already know or between ideas gained through research. Students who are gifted readers will work more effectively when asked to draw information from printed text such as personal accounts of life within the workplace or emailed responses to their questions, scanning and note-taking with ease. Many of the students have talents in other areas (artistic, computer literate, articulate, etc.) which may be utilised effectively when presenting learning. An example of this may be a student with excellent IT skills who can use their experience or knowledge to extend the understanding of the class, such as demonstrating how an IT tool widely used in the workplace can also be used in the classroom. This unit provides opportunities for 'IT experts' to share their email skills or knowledge of conference calling or to utilise their skills to create a slideshow which includes film clips and audio sound bites instead of a more traditional method of presenting their findings.

The World of World

Planner ideas

| **Age group:** 9–12 year olds | **Duration:** 60 hours over approximately 6 weeks |

Unit of inquiry: *The World of Work*

Transdisciplinary theme: *How we organize ourselves*

Central idea: A workplace is a human-made system which serves a purpose.

What is our purpose?
'An inquiry into the interconnectedness of human-made systems and communities; the structure and function of organizations; societal decision-making; economic activities and their impact on humankind and the environment.'
© International Baccalaureate Organization®

Summative assessment ideas

- Ask the students to choose a workplace they have been investigating. Invite them to identify the various roles within that workplace, the skills required from each role, how they interconnect and how they contribute toward achieving the purpose of the organisational workplace.
- As a class, ask the students to identify a project that could come to life in their school (opening a shop at break time, organising a recycling system, etc.).
- Select an example of a purpose that must be achieved; for example, within the school or a place the students are familiar with. Identify all the instances where communication is required and the types of communication that are to be used.
- Ask the students to identify a local workplace in their immediate school environment and the service it provides and the positive and negative impacts it has on the local community and on the environment.
- Suggest the students consider a workplace and think about all the different roles and people who work there. Ask them to make connections between the different departments and how they fit together to provide the overall service.

What do we want to learn?
Form: What are workplaces like?
Function: What are the purposes of a workplace?
Connection: What is the role of workplaces in the local community?
Responsibility: What is the responsibility of a workplace towards the individuals within it?

Lines of inquiry:
- The world of work
- Systems organised to support the workplace
- Interdependence of workplace systems
- Interdependence of the workplace and the local community
- Interdependence of the workplace and the environment
- Roles within the workplace
- How the world of work fulfills needs.

Teacher questions:
- What are 'human-made systems'?
- What are workplaces like?
- What systems are used to organise workplaces?
- What type of communication is needed within a workplace?
- What are different roles within a workplace?
- How do people collaborate at work?
- How are the roles within a workplace interconnected?
- In what ways do workplaces affect the local community?
- In what ways do workplaces affect the environment?

How might we know what we have learned?

Pre-assessment ideas

The students' responses can be recorded in a variety of ways, such as:

- The students can record their answers to each question in the chart on page 15.
- They can conduct a survey of the jobs that their parents do and design a graph or chart to show their results.
- They can cut out and colour the paper figure and thought bubble from the sheet on page 31. They should write the job they might like to do when they grow up in the figure and add the reason why they would like that job in the thought bubble.
- They can use a KWL chart.

Formative assessment ideas

- Ask the students to inquire into jobs they want to find out more about. They can share with the class what they discover.
- Ask the students to prepare tailored questions to interview a guest about their role within a workplace organisation. They can then share the information with the class.
- Arrange the students in groups with a common interest and ask them to write a role-play representing the communication between people within a workplace.
- Invite the students to identify the ultimate purpose of a workplace then investigate the various tasks each person involved in this workplace must carry out in order to help achieve the purpose.

How best might we learn?

Ideas for learning engagements

1 What do your parents do at work?
2 Job questionnaire
3 Going to work
4 Tell me about your job
5 Roles within our school
6 Life-size workers
7 Start your own business
8 Organisations and the environment
9 In my town
10 My future job

Links to the transdisciplinary skills and other attributes

Thinking skills: Identifying parts and relationships between them; drawing meaning from ideas; communicating understanding.

Social skills: Showing respect for all roles; understanding the importance of responsibilities; being courteous in group situations.

Communication skills: Reading sources for information; recording information; speaking clearly; listening to gather information; understanding charts; constructing visuals to share information.

Self-management skills: Planning and carrying out activities effectively; knowing and applying appropriate codes of behaviour.

Research skills: Formulating and asking questions to gather information; sorting information; recording information in a variety of ways.

What resources need to be gathered?

- Books
- Posters & photographs of workplaces
- Resources from the local community, including school staff, parents & locally employed workers
- Cameras
- Audio-visual recording equipment
- DVDs/videos of people at work/interviews with people about their jobs
- ICT resources
- Visits to/guest speakers from local workplaces.

Learner profiles

Inquirers, Communicators, Principled, Reflective.

Class project

Name: _____

Our class project is: _____

Roles	Tasks to complete	Needs to communicate with ...

Name: _____

What will I be?

Cut out this figure and thought bubble. On the figure write what job you would like and in the thought bubble say why this job would suit you.

Name: _____

My school is a workplace

Write in the outer circle some of the roles in your school.

Next write the tasks of that role in the inner circle.

The circle in the centre shows the ultimate purpose of the school.

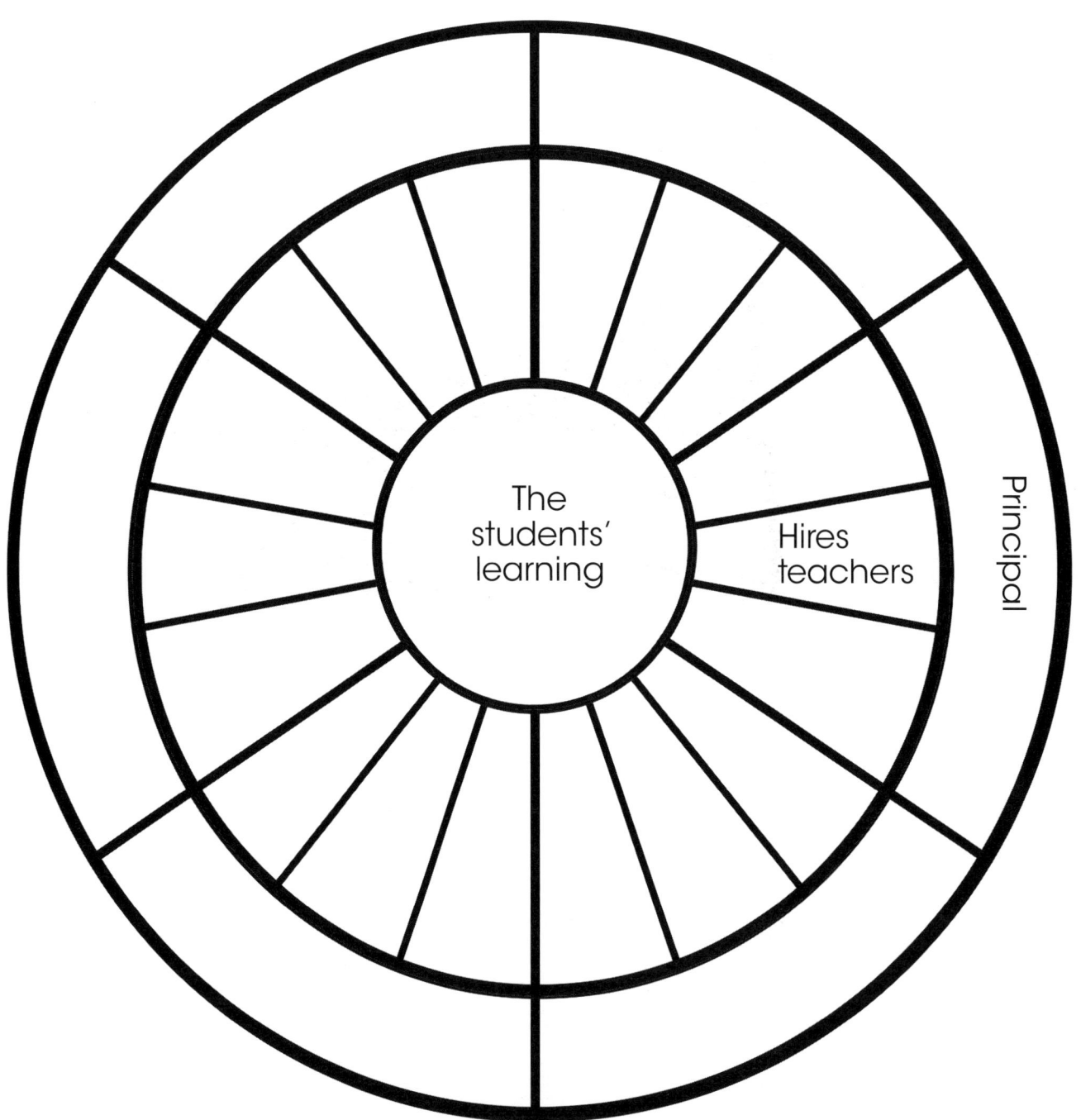